SCUBA SCHOO

D0000181

Night·Limited Visibility Diving

SPECIALTY MANUAL

DISCLAIMER:

The information contained in the SSI training materials is intended to give an individual enrolled in a training course a broad perspective of the diving activity. There are many recommendations and suggestions regarding the use of standard and specialized equipment for the activity. Not all of the equipment discussed in the training material can, or will, be used in this activity. The choice of equipment and techniques used in the course is determined by the location of the activity, the environmental conditions and other factors.

A choice of equipment and techniques cannot be made until the dive site is surveyed immediately prior to the dive. Based on the dive site, the decision should be made regarding which equipment and techniques shall be used. The decision is that of the dive leader *and* the individual enrolled in the training course.

The intent of all SSI training materials is to give individuals as much information as possible in order for individuals to make their own decisions regarding the diving activity, what equipment should be used and what specific techniques may be needed. The ultimate decision on when and how to dive is that of the individual diver.

SCUBA SCHOOLS INTERNATIONAL
2619 Canton Court • Fort Collins, Co 80525-4498
(970) 482-0883 • Fax (970) 482-6157

CONTENTS

ACKNOWLEDGMENTS

Project Manager	**Laurie K. Humpal**
Writer	**Gary R. Clark**
Art Director / Illustrator	**David M. Pratt**
Graphic Designer	**Betsy Musso**
Photographers	**Charlie Arneson** **Blake Miller**
Technical Editors	**Jack Gadbois** **Chris Kralj** **Bert Kobayashi** **Jim Viers**
Proofing Editor	**Linda J. Clark**

READ THIS FIRST

Learning about *Night and Limited Visibility Diving* is fun and convenient. There are four requirements for becoming a comfortable and confident night and limited visibility diver: Knowledge, Skills, Equipment and Experience. These are illustrated by the SSI Diver's Diamond shown here, and are addressed individually below.

KNOWLEDGE

By following the directions below, you can study the academics at home, at your own pace, even if you are not enrolled in a specialty course.

Directions for using the SSI Total Teaching System:

1. **Video** — Watch your SSI *Night & Limited Visibility Diving* video.
2. **Manual** — Read your SSI *Night & Limited Visibility Diving* manual.
3. **Review Questions** — Answer the Chapter Review Questions after each chapter of the manual. Write the answers in your manual.
4. **Answer Sheets** — Transfer the answers to the Answer Sheets. These will be submitted to your Instructor, and retained in your Training Record.

If you are enrolled in a specialty course, your Instructor may also have you take a short exam.

SKILLS

Special *Night and Limited Visibility Diving* skills should be learned in the water, from an Instructor at a professional scuba school run by an SSI Authorized Dealer. You'll learn and practice a variety of techniques, such as using specialized equipment, planning and conducting dives, buddy assistance and emergency situations—all in the open water under an Instructor's guidance and supervision.

EQUIPMENT

For comfortable and enjoyable Night and Limited Visibility diving, specialized equipment is necessary. You will learn about the following equipment in the SSI manual and video:

- Primary Lights
- Secondary Lights
- Strobe Lights
- Surface Lights
- Lines
- Compasses
- Gloves
- Knives
- Whistles

WHILE YOU CAN GAIN KNOWLEDGE THROUGH THIS TEACHING SYSTEM, THE BEST WAY TO BECOME A PROFICIENT NIGHT AND LIMITED VISIBILITY DIVER IS TO ENROLL IN A SPECIALTY COURSE OFFERED BY AN SSI AUTHORIZED DEALER.

EXPERIENCE

Diving experience is essential to becoming a comfortable, confident diver. To measure your experience, SSI has developed ten *Levels of Experience* based on various numbers of dives. For instance, Level 1 is 5 dives, Level 10 is 1000 dives.

Experience is also important in the SSI Education System. To qualify for SSI's *Continuing Education Ratings* (see below) you are required to have a certain Level of Experience, in addition to specialized training.

SSI Continuing Education Made Simple

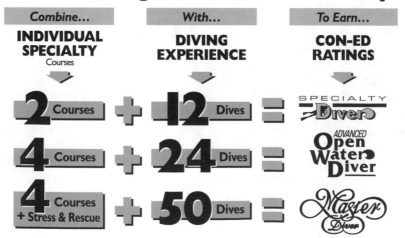

NIGHT VS. LIMITED VISIBILITY DIVING

1

CHAPTER 1:
NIGHT vs. LIMITED VISIBILITY DIVING

In this manual, two types of limited visibility diving will be discussed: that which takes place at night, and that which takes place during the day. Diving at night is considered limited visibility because of the darkness; your vision is confined to the illumination capabilities of your light. Actually, the water itself might be crystal clear, but without lights there would be no visibility at all.

During the day, visibility is restricted because of turbid, or "dirty" water. There are degrees of turbidity, defined in terms of distance. Whether the visibility is any good depends on what is normal for the area

(Figure 1-1). For instance, in some areas 30 feet (9 metres) of "vis" would be considered extremely good, while in others it would be terrible. For most people, limited visibility, or turbid water, is any diving condition with less than 10-15 feet (3-4.5 metres).

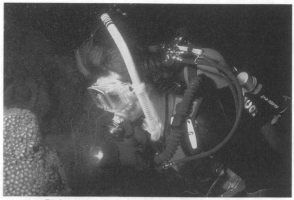

Diving at night is considered limited visibility because of the darkness.

In this manual, the term "Limited Visibility" will mean diving during the daytime in turbid water. Also, "Turbid Water" and "Limited Visibility" will be used interchangeably, and should be understood to mean the same thing. The term "Night Diving" will mean any diving done after dark.

Most of the techniques described in this manual will work

Figure 1-1 *Whether the visibility is any good depends on what is normal for the area.*

for either night diving or limited visibility diving. Night diving is considered a more difficult, advanced condition than limited visibility, requiring more preparation, planning and equipment. The theory is, if you are comfortable diving in nighttime, you will be comfortable diving in limited visibility during the day. Therefore, the techniques described will have a night diving perspective. However, when techniques are unique to either condition, they will be clearly noted as such.

WHAT MAKES WATER TURBID?

The factors creating limited visibility at night are readily apparent. But the factors creating limited visibility during the day are more varied. Before you learn to dive in turbid water, you should first understand what causes it.

Essentially, turbid water is created by particles suspended in the water that block your vision. Water motion is a major contributor to suspended particles. When water moves, it disturbs the particles. Several natural forces cause water to move. Winds on the water's surface create waves, which stir up the water when they "feel" the bottom. Currents are an obvious movement of water. In the spring, run-off from melting snow swells the size of many rivers. This large quantity of fast-moving water collects dirt and debris, which increases the amount of suspended particles in rivers, and the reservoirs and oceans into which they flow. Tidal changes can move massive amounts of water and affect visibility adversely for similar reasons.

There are also living suspended particles. Microscopic algae, collectively called plankton, in sufficient quantity can definitely limit visibility, if not ruin it. An overabundance of certain forms of plankton is known as "red tide."

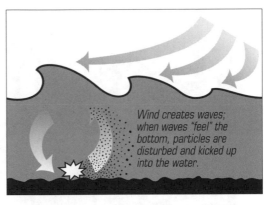

Wind creates waves; when waves "feel" the bottom, particles are disturbed and kicked up into the water.

...turbid water from rivers flows into oceans.

...dirt & debris are pulled into the water from river banks...

Spring snow-melt swells rivers...

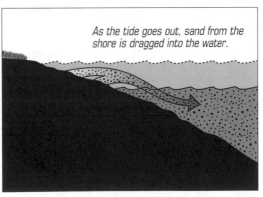

As the tide goes out, sand from the shore is dragged into the water.

Water motion is a major contributor to suspended particles.

Thermoclines, or layers of water with different temperatures, can contribute to limited visibility (Figure 1-2). The colder layers of water tend to trap suspended particles because cold water is denser than warm water. Hence, the velocity of the sinking particles slows down at the thermocline, increasing the concentration along the thermocline.

Figure 1-2   *Thermoclines can contribute to limited visibility.*

Visibility can also become limited by inexperienced divers not practicing neutral buoyancy. Without good neutral buoyancy skills, divers can easily agitate muddy and sandy bottoms with their fin and hand movements, requiring some time for it to settle back down. Preserving visibility is an excellent reason to strive for neutral buoyancy at all times. Kicking coral with your fins or touching it also inflicts harmful damage, potentially killing the coral if it is harmed often enough. The kicked-up sand also has a harmful effect, slowly suffocating the coral as it settles back to the bottom.

Limited Visibility at Night vs. Day
The major similarity between night and turbid water diving is that, in both situations, visibility is reduced. Therefore, many of the techniques will work in either type of limited visibility. But what are the differences? The major contrast is due to a dramatic change of environment—from day to night. Adapting to this change of environment influences every other difference. Take equipment for instance. Night diving requires specialized

underwater lights to compensate for lack of daylight, while in turbid water, lights are simply nice to have (Figure 1-3). Also, night diving requires some additional techniques such as communication, and what to do if your light goes out. Other than that, you will notice only subtle changes in techniques.

Proper, thorough planning and preparation are the keys to minimizing or eliminating any unwanted problems, such as stress. You already have the necessary, fundamental diving skills to dive in limited visibility; all you need to do is acquire some additional skills which are easy and fun to learn. Then, you have only to develop the desire and attitude necessary to expand your diving horizons one step beyond.

Figure 1-3 *Night diving requires specialized underwater lights to compensate for lack of daylight, while in turbid water, lights are simply nice to have.*

UNDERWATER ACTIVITIES

Just because the visibility is limited, it does not mean the opportunities are. Practically any diving activity you can imagine is possible, and some are even exclusive to limited visibility. In fact, learning to dive at night and in turbid water will greatly increase your diving opportunities and enjoyment.

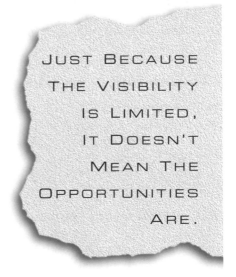

JUST BECAUSE THE VISIBILITY IS LIMITED, IT DOESN'T MEAN THE OPPORTUNITIES ARE.

Night Diving

Diving at night is a natural extension of a diver's activities. Any daytime dive site, no matter how familiar, will be like another world when revisited at night. The contrast of dark water and colorful nocturnal creatures glowing from your dive light create a spectacular, surreal combination.

To many, diving at night is the most exhilarating experience the sport offers. It is stimulating because of the psychological aspect. Being under water in the dark, where you cannot see further than your light source, is absolutely thrilling, both physically and emotionally.

There are a variety of activities you can enjoy while under water at night. Listed below are a few of the more popular ones.

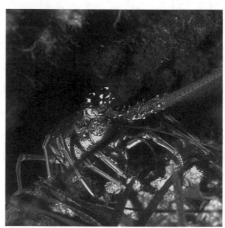

Crustaceans, such as crab, lobster and fresh water crayfish, roam around at night.

■ **Night Life:** Some creatures sleep while others awaken. Crustaceans, such as crab, lobster and fresh water crayfish, roam around feeding; parrot fish sleep under ledges and can be approached; coral polyps, the living creatures inside the hard outer shell, extend their feeding tentacles; bioluminescence, emitted by tiny organisms that glow when the light source is removed, is an entertaining sight. And the colors! The contrast of striking underwater colors surrounded by a black background is truly amazing.

■ **Photography:** As you might imagine, all this makes for unbelievable photographic opportunities. In fact, many people night dive purely for that reason. Just as landscape photographers search for magnificent sunrises and sunsets, underwater photographers search for incredible shots at night. The total absence of filtered light makes for purer color photos with the use of a flash.

■ **Underwater Hunting:** If you are a game collector, nighttime is lobster time. They come out after dark from caves, crevices, and holes to look for food. Not only that, the dive light distracts them and makes them easier to grab. Since entire books have been devoted to the technique of capturing "bugs," the finer points will not be described here. If you want to try your luck at game collecting, check the seasons, game limits, size restrictions, and local laws before taking anything. Also, be aware that, depending on your location, some species are not allowed to be taken at night, or while on scuba.

Limited Visibility

Limited visibility may be the most common, readily available condition for most divers. It encompasses a diverse range of diving activities, conditions, and potential sites such as the kelp beds of California or the wrecks of the Great Lakes, New Jersey and North Carolina. Many inland lakes and rivers also offer excellent limited visibility experiences (Figure 1-4). There are so many different activities, such as spearfishing, photography, underwater archaeology, exploring and navigating that, more than likely, there are dive sites nearby where you could have an underwater adventure.

Figure 1-4 *Many inland lakes and rivers also offer excellent limited visibility experiences.*

For many divers, exotic tropical getaways are where they dream of going, but local areas are where they actually dive. To enhance the experience, many inland divers combine diving with other activities, such as biking, wind surfing, jet and water skiing (Figure 1-5). For them, the overall social exchange, in addition to

Figure 1-5 *To enhance the experience, many inland divers combine diving with other activities, such as water skiing.*

the diving, make the trip more than worthwhile. It depends on where you live, your affection for the sport, how often you want to participate, and the people you want to participate with.

■ **Underwater Hunting:** Two challenging activities are spearfishing and game collecting. In the early years of scuba, underwater hunting was the main reason people went diving. In certain regions of the U.S., it is still extremely popular. There is a wide variety of game, from clams, crawfish and walleye in fresh water, to lobster, abalone and grouper in salt water. Before participating, check the local license requirements, legal seasons, and size limitations with the local professional dive store.

■ **Underwater Exploring:** Another obvious activity is underwater exploring. Many people become very familiar with a local body of water. They find fascinating underwater formations and uncover unknown geologic occurrences. Some take it to extremes, working with local fish and game authorities mapping fish migratory patterns, tagging fish, and studying spawning seasons.

■ **Navigation:** Besides using their skills to navigate during the dive, many divers use their skills in competitions. They set up underwater courses of varying difficulty to see who can perform the best, or search for objects planted along a predefined course. The games are a test of accuracy and skill that many enjoy, and they add a new dimension to diving, especially in limited visibility.

■ **Wreck Diving:** An extension of underwater exploring is wreck diving (Figure 1-6). In many parts of the world, wreck diving is exceptionally popular. Imagine seeing a ship under water much larger than the boat you came on. There are wreck dives for divers of all abilities, located in shallow to dangerously deep water. It

Figure 1-6 *An extension of underwater exploring is wreck diving.*

is not recommended for sport divers to penetrate wrecks. This requires a great deal of additional training and experience. However, to learn the basics, SSI offers a Wreck Diving specialty course that will get you started.

■ **Underwater Archaeology:** An area of the sport that is rapidly gaining popularity is underwater archaeology. Several areas of the country are establishing underwater parks devoted to shipwrecks. Many of these parks were built thanks to the efforts of local sport divers. Also, it is possible to participate on scientific archeological studies. A number of important projects rely heavily on sport divers who volunteer their time.

■ **Personal Challenges:** If you are the type of person who enjoys personal challenges, diving where you cannot see more than a few feet (metres) is an excellent activity. It is like constantly looking around a new corner; a new world is unveiled every few feet (metres). There is also the aspect of sensory deprivation, or being under water where you cannot see far, hear much, smell anything, or feel as you normally do. Under those circumstances, your senses are dulled, but your awareness is amplified to compensate. This heightened state of awareness is exhilarating. For that reason, many people dive in limited visibility not so much for what they can *see,* but for how it makes them *feel.* It is just a different kind of diving, a different sort of thrill, requiring a different attitude and skills.

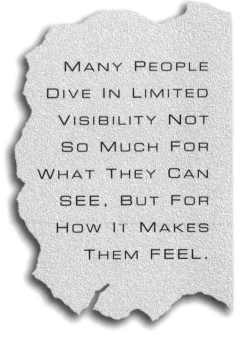

MANY PEOPLE DIVE IN LIMITED VISIBILITY NOT SO MUCH FOR WHAT THEY CAN SEE, BUT FOR HOW IT MAKES THEM FEEL.

CHAPTER 1
REVIEW

1. Diving at night is considered _____ _____ because of the darkness; your vision is confined to the illumination capabilities of your light.

2. "_____ _____" and "_____ _____" will be used interchangeably, and should be understood to mean the same thing.

3. Essentially, _____ _____ is created by particles suspended in the water that block your vision.

4. _____, or layers of water with different temperatures, can contribute to limited visibility.

5. Preserving visibility is an excellent reason to strive for _____ _____ at all times.

SPECIAL EQUIPMENT

2

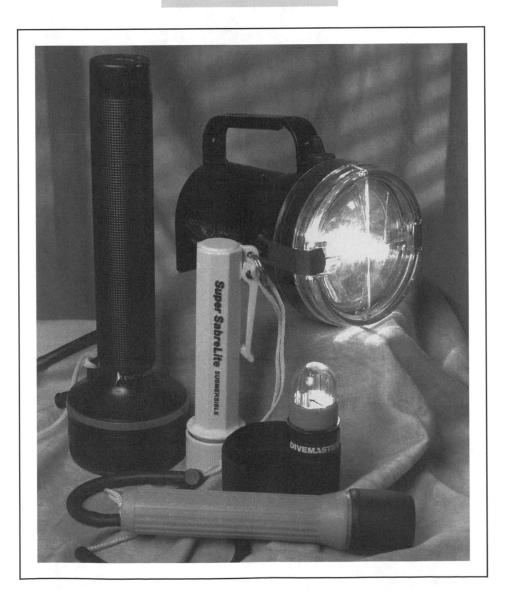

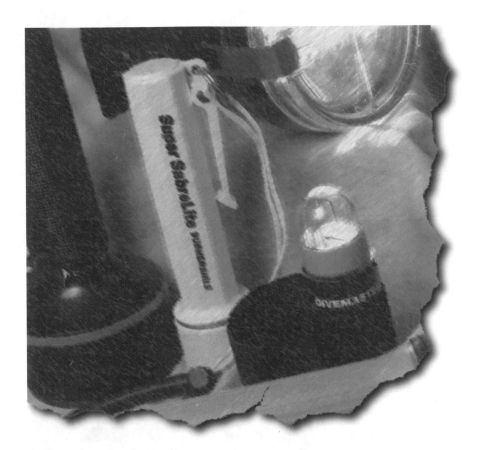

CHAPTER 2:
SPECIAL
EQUIPMENT

Any specialized diving activity requires specialized equipment. It is the nature of the sport, and night and limited visibility diving are not exceptions. Lights, knives, and compasses are a few pieces of gear used by experienced divers.

In this chapter you will learn about the special equipment used on night and limited visibility dives that enhances safety and comfort. When you finish, you should know what additional equipment is required, and the purpose, usage and features of that equipment. For more information on equipment, see your local SSI retailer about enrolling in an SSI Equipment specialty course.

UNDERWATER LIGHTS

Underwater lights are of primary concern to night divers because they are the only source of light during the dive, however, they are also valuable to limited visibility divers. This section covers the different types of lights, their features, selecting and maintaining them, along with their purpose on both types of dives. The use of lights during the dive will be covered in Chapter 4.

Night Diving

There are four main types of underwater lights used on night dives: primary, secondary, chemical, and strobe. There are also a variety of accessory lights. Each has a particular application during the dive.

Diving Lights.

■ **Primary:** Primary lights are the diver's main light source. Usually, they are the largest, brightest lights taken on the dive. There are various designs, from the standard flashlight, to lamp or pistol grip, to an angular handle.

■ **Secondary:** Secondary lights are backup (safety) lights, that are used when primary lights fail. Underwater lights, being mechanical devices, are not immune to problems. Batteries and bulbs can fail, and o-rings can leak, so safety conscious divers prepare for the light failure situation by keeping a secondary light in their BC pocket, or strapping it someplace accessible. This allows a diver to switch immediately to another light source, minimizing his exposure to blackouts. Blackouts, or the absence of light under water, are unnerving and should be avoided if possible. Exact procedures for using a secondary light and dealing with light failure under water are described in Chapter 4: The Dive.

■ **Locator Lights:** In night diving, locator lights are mainly used to mark divers, ascent/descent lines, ladders, boats, and buoys. The two common types of locator lights are chemical lights and reusable flares. Chemical lights contain liquid chemicals that, when mixed, produce a bright glow. However, some areas now ban the use of chemical lights for environmental reasons. Reusable flares provide the same function, but use batteries instead of chemicals. It is highly recommended that every night diver attach a locator light to his or her tank valve or regulator hose (Figure 2-1).

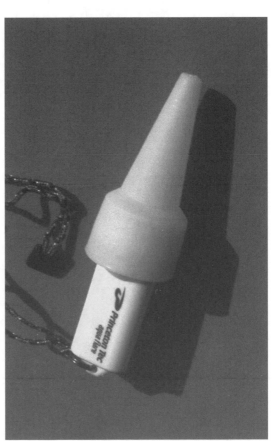

Figure 2-1 *It is highly recommended that every night diver attach a locator light to his or her tank valve or regulator hose.*

■ **Strobe:** Strobes look like small dive lights, but flash in rhythmic intervals rather than having a fixed beam. They are attached to lines, ladders, boats, and buoys, making them easier to locate under water. They are not normally attached to divers because they are too distracting.

■ **Accessory:** Accessory lights either act as the primary light, or provide light in addition to the primary unit. Some attach to regulator hoses, consoles or equipment straps. Others attach to masks or have headbands, so the light is aimed wherever the diver looks, similar to a miner's headlamp.

Limited Visibility

During the daytime, underwater lights are valuable for restoring color and light at depth. As you descend in limited visibility, natural light dissipates and, at some point, it may become very dark. This happens because the suspended particles that block your vision also block the sun's ability to penetrate the water. This loss of color occurs in a predictable sequence (Figure 2-2). Red disappears in the first 10 feet (3 metres); orange and yellow disappear next—usually within 30 feet (9 metres). Green is one of the last colors to disappear (at around 60 feet or 18 metres), leaving everything with a blue tinge at this depth. When lighter colors such as yellow disappear, they become pale and off-white. Darker colors, such as red or violet, appear blue or black. By using an underwater light, you can reignite the explosion of color that the water seems to suppress.

Figure 2-2 *Water absorbs light as it passes through, and color fades increasingly as you descend. This loss of color occurs in a predictable sequence.*

Lights with wide, medium-bright beams work best, because they highlight a wider area with softer light. The softer light provides plenty of light, because you are interested only in illuminating objects close to you. As you will use the light for color restoration, not for vision or safety, one light should be sufficient.

Features of Underwater Lights

True underwater lights are designed to withstand underwater pressure. There are many water resistant lights that are sealed against moisture, but they do not hold up under pressure at depth. Because the importance of a reliable light source cannot be stressed enough, only lights designed for diving should be used.

All lights should be equipped with a lanyard, which is a strap connected to the light that also goes around your wrist (Figure 2-3). That way, if you let go of the light during your dive, you can retrieve it easily. The lanyard should have a fastening mechanism to close the strap snugly around your wrist. Its length should allow the light to go no further than approximately 6 inches (15 centimetres) out of reach. A clip on the lanyard is handy if the diver requires some type of hands-free activity because the light can be clipped to some other piece of equipment.

Normally, the brightness of underwater lights is measured in candlepower or watts. In terms of candlepower, lights range in brightness from 4 to 100,000 or more. This measurement describes the amount of light emitted by an equal number of burn-

Figure 2-3   *All lights should be equipped with a lanyard, which is a strap connected to the light that also goes around your wrist.*

ing candles. In terms of watts, lights range in brightness from around 4 to 25. Wattage on dive lights is not related to wattage of ordinary house bulbs. Be aware that any measurement of brightness is somewhat deceptive because, usually, the measurement is made on land at the brightest point of the bulb's filament. Because water is so dense, the brightness tends to degrade as the light passes through the lens and into the water.

Brightness is also affected by the power supply of the light. A light needs to have adequate, appropriate power for the wattage of the bulb. A bulb having high wattage, but driven by an insufficient battery is not as bright as one with adequate power. However, the power supply should not be too powerful for the bulb or it will burn out quickly. As a rule of thumb, the more batteries, the longer the light will last, but the light will also be larger. A desirable compromise exists between the size, weight, and brightness. The goal is to be as small, bright, and long-lasting as possible.

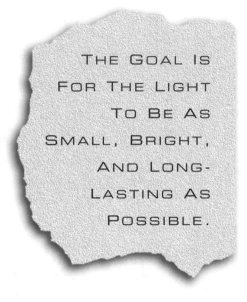

THE GOAL IS FOR THE LIGHT TO BE AS SMALL, BRIGHT, AND LONG-LASTING AS POSSIBLE.

The dimension of the light's beam is as important as its brightness because it defines the light's usefulness. Most lights emit either narrow or wide beams. A narrow beam will concentrate bright light on the small area it illuminates, and can throw the beam a long distance. A wider beam will illuminate a larger area with less intense light in a single spot.

Underwater lights have two types of power sources: rechargeable or replaceable batteries. Both have advantages and disadvantages, depending on your needs. The power source can be contained within the light, or remote and connected to the light with a cord.

■ **Rechargeable Batteries:** Lights with rechargeable batteries are mostly used as primary lights, and are favored by those who use them frequently. The advantage is that they are brighter than non-rechargeable batteries, and new batteries are not purchased for each dive. Instead, a 110V current recharges the nickel-cadmium (nicad) or lead-acid (Gel-cell) batteries through an adapter (Figure 2-4). Even though they are initially more expensive than other lights, rechargeables will pay off in the long run through savings in replacement batteries. The disadvantage is that the power supply does not last as long as fresh, replaceable batteries do. The other problem is that it can take up to 12 or 15 hours to recharge the batteries. Also, some countries do not use 110-volt current, so a converter is required for charging.

■ **Non-rechargeable Batteries:** Lights with non-rechargeable batteries are excellent primary or secondary lights, and make a lot of sense for divers who use them infrequently. The advantage is that they are initially less expensive and you only buy batteries when you use the light. Battery sizes range from large 6-volt to small AA cell, and the number of batteries required depends on the power of the light. With fresh batteries, the power tends to last longer than rechargeable batteries. The disadvantage is that the batteries should be replaced before each night dive to ensure they will last for the duration of the dive. These lights may not be as

Figure 2-4 *A 110V current recharges the batteries through an adapter.*

intense as a rechargeable battery either. On dive trips to foreign countries, you may also need to bring your own supply of batteries because there is no guarantee you will find the right size or quantity at a reasonable price.

Selecting Underwater Lights

When purchasing a dive light, first think about your needs (Figure 2-5). If you plan on using it a lot, you should consider a rechargeable light. On the other hand, if you do not plan on using it often, one with replaceable batteries is probably better.

The best way to test a light's brightness is to use it under water on a dive, or at least in a fill tank in the store. Shining it off a wall in the store is an inaccurate judge of its capabilities.

Figure 2-5 *When purchasing a dive light, first think about your needs.*

The important features are underwater brightness, overall compactness, quantity and cost of batteries needed, how many hours the beam is sustained, as well as ease of maintenance. Although the list is long, by keeping all these things in mind when shopping, you increase your chances of selecting the best light for your needs.

Maintaining Underwater Lights

To ensure their continued reliability, you have to maintain lights properly (Figure 2-6). Along with improved reliability, regular maintenance also extends the life of dive lights.

Maintenance is easy and only takes a few minutes. The goal is to prevent leaks and guarantee continuous, uninter-

Figure 2-6   *To ensure their continued reliability, you have to maintain lights properly*

rupted light during the dive. The procedure includes checking the batteries, the bulb, the watertight seal, the electrical connections, and the light switch. In addition, check the lanyard frequently.

■ **Batteries:** Without new or freshly charged batteries, you cannot guarantee that the light will last the entire dive. At night, light failure is something you definitely want to avoid. During the day it is more of an inconvenience. Remember that rechargeable batteries can take up to 12 or 15 hours to charge.

■ **Watertight Seal:** Inspect the o-rings for wear. They are usually found in the lens seal. Remove them carefully and wipe them clean with a soft cloth. They should be smooth and flawless, without depressions, cuts or cracks. Next, using your fingertips, lubricate the o-ring with clear silicone grease (Figure 2-7). Apply a thin coating

Figure 2-7   *Lubricate the o-ring with clear silicone grease.*

on the entire o-ring, but not an excessive amount. Too much grease actually inhibits proper sealing and collects sand and dirt. The proper amount of grease will leave the o-ring shiny, without any unwanted globs. Before replacing the o-ring, wipe the space where it fits clean with a cotton swab.

■ **Bulb:** There are two main types of bulbs: Krypton and Halogen. If the filament is detached, you should replace the bulb with one of the same size and wattage. Filaments are the small wires inside the glass. Also, be aware that these bulbs can get very hot, so avoid touching them after a light has been switched on. Finally, due to the heat the bulbs create, oil from your fingers could cause premature failure. Carefully wipe them clean after replacing, or use a tissue to avoid direct contact.

■ **Electrical Connections:** Inspect the contact points of both the power source and bulb. They should be clean and free of corrosion. If corrosion exists, it inhibits the free flow of electricity, while extensive corrosion may prevent the light from working at all. Gently buff contact points with very fine sandpaper or steel wool, or rub them with a rough cloth or pencil eraser.

Gently buff contact points to keep them free of corrosion.

■ **Light Switch:** Some lights have rubber boots over the switch. If the rubber is not in good condition, water could leak into the light. Cracks and holes in the rubber need to be fixed by a professional dive store.

After the inspection, reassemble the light carefully and turn it on. It should have a steady, bright beam of white light. A dull, yellow beam means the battery is low. If it does not work at all, check the battery connections, make sure the lamp is secure in the socket, and that the filament is not broken. If you cannot find the problem, take the light to your local SSI dive store for service.

SURFACE LIGHTS (NIGHT DIVING)

During a night dive, you will need light for dressing and entering the water. Using your primary light for dressing wastes the batteries. In addition, you will need light to show you the way back to the exit point on shore. These needs are met by a surface light.

The most effective surface lights are either gas lanterns or flashing lights (Figure 2-8). Gas lanterns are the brightest lights for their size, are very reliable, and also provide light when dressing. Flashing lights are easily spotted from the water, but do not provide enough light for dressing. At some sites, street lights provide excellent surface lighting, or there may even be a permanent light at popular beaches or resorts. Procedures for setting up lights on the shore or boat are covered in Chapter 4.

Figure 2-8   *The most effective surface lights are either gas lanterns or flashing lights.*

LINES

Lines are extremely valuable to night and limited visibility divers (Figure 2-9). They are used mostly for descending, ascending and safety stops. If you are diving from a boat, the most common is the anchor line. Some boats also have drop lines, which are weighted lines attached to the boat and dropped down into the water. Drop bars, which are bars that hang horizontally 15 to 20 feet (4.5 to 6 metres) below the surface, work well for safety stops, but not for descents and ascents. Most commercial dive boats have some combination of one or more of these lines available.

If you are diving from shore, some lines may be available for use. In protected diving spots, floats are often used to mark the boundaries of the diving area. These floats are attached with lines that can be used by divers. If no pre-existing floats and lines are available at the dive site, you can bring your own. You can

Figure 2-9   *Lines are valuable to night and limited visibility divers.*

carry a dive flag or some other type of float and use the attached line. In most states and countries, dive flags are not only required by law, but are a necessary safety precaution when diving during the day. Flags that are visible at night are becoming popular as well.

When setting your own float and line, it should be able to withstand adverse conditions, such as strong currents, windy and wavy conditions. To accomplish that, the weight anchoring the flag or float must be heavy enough to keep the object from being swept away. Also, the line should be strong enough to maintain the float and weight connection. A strong but inexpensive line is 1/4 inch (6mm) polypropylene, which is commonly a yellow color. In addition, the float should have

A float and line for shore divers.

sufficient buoyancy to hold you up, if necessary, with full dive equipment. If a dive flag is attached to the float, it should conform to the regulations of the area you are diving in. In addition, it should be large enough to be visible from at least 100 feet (30 metres), and should have a mechanism to hold it out for view.

COMPASS

A compass is also extremely valuable, either during the day or at night. In limited visibility water, your distance vision is restricted, making it difficult to see "the big picture." Because of this, natural navigation is hampered. Natural navigation is the art of using underwater landmarks and topography to find your way around. A compass helps compensate by indicating the direction, and allowing you to follow a heading from point A to point B and back. When used properly, compasses give divers the ability to enter the water, make the dive, and swim back where they started, without surfacing for directions. Navigation is covered in Chapter 5: Advanced Techniques.

Underwater compass

A good underwater compass will have several features. It will be large, clearly marked, and easy to read. It will also have a lubber line, which is a fixed line attached to the face of the compass, designating the direction you swim. In addition, it will have a moveable bezel with degree markings. Most important, it will have a magnetic needle that points north. Other features are a luminous dial, so the markings can be read in low light, and an oil-filled housing.

GLOVES

Gloves help protect your hands and fingers. In limited visibility conditions you cannot always see everything you are touching. There may be some hidden, sharp object such as a broken bottle or fishing lure. At night, some stinging marine life may not be easily visible. An example is the sea urchin which is black and spiny. Touching one with bare hands may cause an immediate sharp pain from the brittle spines. Gloves help prevent this from happening. Of course, you should not touch coral and other delicate marine life that is easily seen and avoided.

Most gloves that are used in cold water are made of neoprene. The thickness you need will depend on the temperature of the water, and the level of protection you desire. Reef gloves are usually made of a thin neoprene, synthetic leather, or a rubberized material and are good for diving in warmer, tropical waters.

KNIFE

A knife becomes extremely useful when entanglement occurs. Fishing line, nets, and kelp are potential problems for divers in limited visibility. Fin strap buckles, instrument consoles, and other dangling equipment are also likely to become snagged. Streamlining your equipment will reduce the incidence of snagging. Also, banging your knife on your tank is an effective means of communication under water.

A good dive knife is sharp and will have a serrated edge. The knife should come out of the sheath easily, but not fall out accidentally. It should be easily accessible, usually placed on the leg, on the back of your console, or attached to the BC. A large knife is not necessary, but the blade should be large enough to cut a piece of rope, for example. Remember, the knife is a tool, not a weapon.

ADDITIONAL EQUIPMENT

One other piece of equipment will enhance the safety of your dive. By carrying a whistle, you can signal for help from quite a distance—much farther than you can shout. The whistle should be easily accessible, so you can use it in case of an emergency. Many divers hook the whistle to their BC hoses.

Another equipment tip will help you read instruments in turbid water. Take a small plastic bag filled with clear water. Place the bag over the gauge face and it will be easier to read. Some divers put the instruments inside the water-filled bag and close it around the hose. You must secure the bag tightly so dirty water does not mix with the clear water.

With a few additional pieces of equipment, night and limited visibility diving can be more fun. Actually, everything listed above is considered standard dive equipment. The difference is, in many types of diving not all this equipment is absolutely necessary. In limited visibility, it is. So, before you dive in turbid water or at night, make sure you have all the proper equipment.

CHAPTER 2
REVIEW

1. Underwater _____ are of primary concern to night divers because they are the only source of _____ during the dive.

2. Secondary _____ are backup (safety) lights, that are used when _____ _____ fail.

3. It is highly recommended that every night diver attach a _____ _____ to his or her tank valve or regulator hose.

4. There are many _____ _____ lights that are sealed against moisture, but they do not hold up under pressure at depth.

5. All lights should be equipped with a _____, which is a strap connected to the light that also goes around your wrist.

6. Underwater lights have two types of power sources: _____ or _____ batteries.

7. The proper amount of grease will leave the ____ – _____ shiny, without unwanted globs.

8. _____ _____ are the brightest lights for their size, are very reliable, and also provide light when dressing.

PREPARING TO DIVE

3

CHAPTER 3:
PREPARING
TO DIVE

Diving at night or in limited visibility requires total preparation because there is little room for error. This means your equipment must be reliable and trouble free, and you should be in the right emotional and physical condition as well. Preparedness requires careful and thorough planning, so that you can anticipate and be ready for any potential problems.

In your Open Water Diver course, you learned the fundamentals of dive preparation. This chapter will build on that foundation, while furthering your knowledge of dive planning and getting yourself and your equipment ready. When you finish, you will know how to organize an enjoyable dive.

MAKING A DIVE PLAN

There are several key stages of dive planning. First, you must decide where you want to go and what you want to do on the dive. Sometimes the activity will dictate the choice of dive sites. Underwater hunting and photography are activities that directly influence where you dive. Other times, the site, such as a wreck, will be the main focus of the dive.

After setting your objective, the remaining parameters of the dive can be filled in at the site. The complete dive plan should cover all the parameters discussed below.

Dive planning is an important part of night/limited visibility diving.

Selecting a Dive Site

Any dive site should be suited to your ability, as well as the level of your experience. New divers should not attempt advanced sites. Experienced divers should decide whether they feel like a challenge or something relaxing just for fun.

When selecting a site that has limited visibility, the major considerations are depth, entry/exit points, surf, currents and, of course, your ability, experience and desire to handle each one.

■ **Depth:** The site should not be excessively deep. It is unnecessary to dive deep when visibility is limited, because the light disappears quickly at depth, compounding the visibility difficulties.

■ **Entry/Exit Points:** When diving from shore, look for a site that allows easy, safe access to and from the water. Avoid places where you have to climb down and up steep rocks or negotiate sharp submerged rocks and reefs (Figure 3-1). These spots are difficult during the daylight and very dangerous at night, especially with heavy tanks and weight belts. When diving from a boat, there may be objects under water you cannot see from above. Be sure that you can exit the water as safely as you can enter it.

Figure 3-1   *Avoid entry points with sharp or submerged rocks.*

■ **Surf:** Even on sandy beaches, avoid heavy surf. Large waves are difficult enough during the daytime, and even more hazardous at night. Watch the surf for a long enough period so you can see the entire spectrum of wave sizes.

■ **Currents:** You must be aware of rip currents and longshore currents when diving from shore. Also, check the local tide tables to avoid diving during an undesirable tidal change.

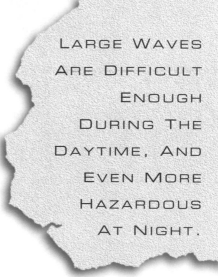

LARGE WAVES ARE DIFFICULT ENOUGH DURING THE DAYTIME, AND EVEN MORE HAZARDOUS AT NIGHT.

Night Diving Site Considerations

Selecting a site is critical for night diving because the planning is very site-dependent. The site should be one you have dived during the daytime, preferably on a day similar in conditions to your night dive. Here are a few more considerations particular to night diving:

■ **Visibility:** Night diving in very turbid water is a tough challenge. Normally, it is not a good idea, unless you are very familiar with the dive site. The main reason is that night diving can be disorienting even in clear water, and can be more disorienting in turbid water.

■ **Facilities for Changing:** Unless you are diving where it is warm at night, it is important to have some place to change and get warm after the dive (Figure 3-2). Changing out of the wet suit is more of a concern than a dry suit. Hypothermia after the dive is always possible, if there is no place to get warm, especially at night.

Figure 3-2   *It is important to have some place to change and get warm after the dive.*

■ **Cold Water:** If you night dive in cold water, make sure to have the proper exposure suit. Night diving under the ice is beyond the scope of sport diving and this course, and should not be attempted.

■ **Weather:** A calm, clear night is best for night diving, particularly if the moon is full and bright. Be aware that run-offs from heavy rains often create strong currents and reduce water clarity dramatically. Heavy rain and extreme cold are unpleasant conditions that hamper the dive, but can be overcome by adventurous enthusiasts. Dangerous conditions like lightning should cause you to call off the dive.

Planning The Dive

Making a dive plan forces you to consider all aspects of the dive, which is the key to safety and comfort. The planning process is shared responsibility between buddies, and if you are in a

Planning the dive as a group makes for a fun, social exchange.

group, all buddy teams should participate. This makes dive planning a fun, social exchange, which is one of the most enjoyable aspects of diving.

The components of a good night or limited visibility dive plan are listed below.

■ **Goal:** The goal of the dive is the reason you are making the dive. Different goals will require different kinds of dive plans.

■ **Maximum Depth:** It is recommended to dive relatively shallow on either night or limited visibility dives because light dissipates quickly, meaning there is very little visibility at depth.

■ **Maximum Bottom Time:** Whatever maximum bottom time is selected, you and your buddy should agree not to exceed it.

■ **Minimum Air Supply:** Air management is even more important in limited visibility or at night, therefore, responsible divers surface with no less than 500 PSI (35 BAR) air pressure. The "rule of thirds" is also typical, where you use one-third of your air for the swim out, one-third for the swim back, and one-third for emergencies.

■ **Lighting:** Make sure all key locations are marked with lights, and that you have a fully charged primary and secondary light.

■ **Handling Contingencies:** A contingency particular to night diving is the loss-of-light situation. The recommended procedure for the loss-of-light situation will be discussed in Chapter 4. Remember to designate one buddy as the team leader who would have responsibilities for keeping track of maximum depth, minimum pressure, and direction. The other buddy should always remain on the same side of the team leader during the dive to minimize the chance of separation.

When you make a dive plan, it does not mean you need to be a slave to it, especially if you allow a comfortable safety margin. When stretching a dive plan, use caution with respect to your dive profile and keep in mind that you can extend the depth and time, but not your air supply.

Once the dive plan is made, you should tell someone else about it so they will know where you are going, what you are doing, and when to expect you back (Figure 3-3). This could save your life if an emergency occurs, because the authorities will know where to look if you have not returned by the designated time. If you decide to spend time somewhere else, be sure to notify your friends of where you expect to dive.

Figure 3-3   *You should tell someone else where you are going, what you are doing and when to expect you back.*

TOPSIDE PERSONNEL

Although it is not always practical, you should try to find someone willing to stay on shore or in the boat while you and your buddy dive. If you are shore diving, the person should watch the surface light, your equipment, and the weather. If you are boat diving, the person should not only watch the surface light and the weather, but also know how to drive the boat, run the anchor system and use the radio, if available. These people are invaluable for keeping your things on shore from being stolen, helping you get into and out of the water, and being there if you have an emergency.

PREPARING YOUR EQUIPMENT

Before you go diving, make sure you have all the equipment you need and that it works and fits properly. The steps for basic equipment preparation are listed below:

■ **Go Through Equipment Checklist:** To ensure you have all your equipment, see the checklist in the appendix for a standard dive equipment set. It is inconvenient to arrive at the dive site only to discover you forgot to pack a piece of equipment.

■ **Inspect Your Equipment for Problems:** Replace damaged or worn straps, lubricate wet suit zippers, repair torn wet suits, and make sure all your equipment works well and is adjusted properly (Figure 3-4).

Figure 3-4   *Make sure all your equipment works well and is adjusted properly.*

■ **Have a Professional Service Your Equipment:** Regulators, alternate air sources, power inflators, depth gauges and submersible pressure gauges should be serviced at your local professional dive store at least once per year, or as recommended by the manufacturer. These pieces of equipment are your life support, so make sure they work properly. After that, use them in a pool to ensure they are adjusted and work satisfactorily.

■ **Prepare a Spare Parts and Repair Kit:** The spare parts and repair kit is essential. Check with your local dive store for special recommendations, but be sure to include extra mask straps, fin straps, snorkel keepers, and tank o-rings in all popular sizes. Also include mask defog. A suggested kit is listed in the Appendix. Nothing is more disappointing than arriving at a spectacular dive site, having a minor equipment problem and not being able to fix it.

■ **Purchase New or Specialized Equipment:** If something is old or worn out, it could be a good time to replace it. If you have been thinking about completing your scuba set, look seriously at purchasing that missing component. Now that you are in the Night / Limited Visibility Diving specialty course, it is the ideal opportunity to purchase lights and other equipment required for this aspect of the sport. Even if you already have all the basic equipment, there are many fun accessories that keep diving interesting and add new flavor to the sport.

■ **Mark All Equipment With Your Name:** Use a waterproof marker and write your name or initials on every piece of equipment, including bags and dry boxes (Figure 3-5). Be sure to mark your equipment in a conspicuous spot. On a crowded shore or boat, it is likely that somebody will have the same equipment you have. Marking your equipment beforehand avoids questions about ownership.

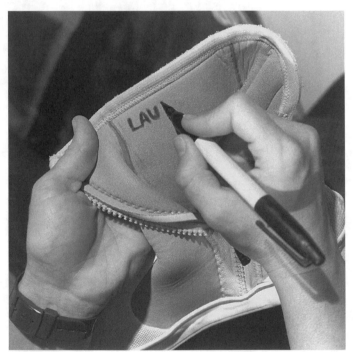

Figure 3-5   *To prevent loss, write your name or initials on every piece of equipment.*

The best way to take care of your equipment is to complete the SSI Equipment Techniques specialty course. You will learn how equipment works, how to maintain your own equipment and make basic field repairs, and to become a wiser, more informed equipment purchaser.

GETTING YOURSELF READY

It is as important to prepare yourself for diving as it is your equipment. Being in good physical and mental condition before a dive allows you to get the most from the dive. Also, divers in good shape are more confident and better able to adapt to difficult environmental conditions and emergency situations (Figure 3-6).

Figure 3-6 *Divers in good shape are more confident.*

A variety of sports and aerobic exercises are excellent preparation for diving because they strengthen leg muscles and provide a cardiovascular workout. These would include:

- Running and walking
- Swimming
- Swimming with fins
- Bicycling (stationary and on the road)
- Aerobics
- Snorkeling

Of course, do not forget to eat healthy food. Eating right is as important as exercise. Before diving, plan to eat light foods that are easily digested. Avoid spicy foods that produce stomach gas. It is also important to get adequate sleep before a dive and, as always, never drink alcohol or take drugs before diving.

AS ALWAYS, NEVER DRINK ALCOHOL OR TAKE DRUGS BEFORE DIVING.

SCUBA SKILLS UPDATE

When diving at night or in limited visibility, it is very important to be comfortable in the water and with your equipment; so if you have not been diving in a year or more, you should strongly consider an SSI *Scuba Skills Update* program. This program is designed to refresh your basic diving skills and raise your personal comfort and confidence. Available at your local SSI Authorized Dealer, it is the ideal way to brush up on your diving skills and, most importantly, maintain your proficiency as a diver.

MONITORING THE DIVE SITE

Before a night dive, you should monitor the site during the day (Figure 3-7). The weather, surf and other conditions can change and worsen, perhaps to the extent that you will want to call off the dive. Although it is not always practical, monitoring the site can save time and trouble—if you realize that you should call off the dive before hauling equipment to the site.

Figure 3-7   *Before a night dive, you should monitor the site during the day.*

There are several ways to keep track of the conditions. You can check the site from shore or from a boat, depending on your resources and where the site is. For shore dives, driving by the site works well if it is near a road. It is a good idea to stop the car when inspecting the conditions. For boat dives, going by the spot during the day is a good idea if you have a private boat. On chartered boats, the captain will determine if the conditions are favorable.

If the site is unfamiliar to you or your buddy, it is highly recommended that at least one of you dive the site during the day prior to the night dive. This is a good idea for several reasons. It helps you determine the best entry/exit points and gives you a feel for the underwater terrain. This knowledge will also improve your natural navigation abilities. You should determine the site's depth, and look for underwater hazards such as fishing nets that are difficult to see at night, because entanglement is never a good situation under water, and is even more dangerous at night. You and your buddy will have a much better experience simply by knowing what to expect from the dive.

Night and limited visibility diving do not require much more preparation than other types of diving, but it must be thorough preparation. It just makes sense that when your vision is limited, you should take extra precautionary steps. This means making a complete dive plan that includes selecting an appropriate dive site for your ability, and diligently preparing yourself and your equipment. With planning and preparation, you can enjoy the wonders of night and limited visibility diving.

With planning and preparation, you can enjoy the wonders of night and limited visibility diving.

CHAPTER 3
REVIEW

1. Any dive site should be suited to your ability, as well as the level of your _____. New divers should not attempt advanced sites.

2. It is unnecessary to dive _____ when visibility is limited, because the light disappears quickly at depth, compounding the visibility difficulties.

3. Selecting a site is critical for night diving because the planning is very site-dependent. The site should be one you have _____ during the _____, preferably on a day similar in conditions to your night dive.

4. Dangerous conditions like _____ should cause you to call off the dive.

5. Make sure all key locations are marked with _____, and that you have a fully charged primary and secondary light.

6. If the site is _____ to you or your buddy, it is highly recommended that at least one of you dive the site during the day prior to the night dive.

THE DIVE

4

CHAPTER 4:
THE DIVE

Descending in water with limited visibility is a completely exhilarating feeling, especially the first time you do it. There is a rush of adrenaline, followed by a sense of discovery when you see the bottom. If the dive is at night, it will be a consuming adventure. If it is during the day, every few feet will reveal something new. A small area can seem larger than it is.

In this chapter, you will learn to put the preparation and dive planning process into action. You will apply the basic techniques from your Open Water Diver class, and learn additional techniques. When you are done, you will understand the fundamentals of entering the water, conducting a dive, and exiting the water. This chapter will focus on night diving because it is a more technical dive to conduct. However, the differences in daytime limited visibility diving are also addressed.

SETTING UP SURFACE LIGHTS (NIGHT DIVING)

When night diving, the first step is to set up the surface lights (Figure 4-1). It is critical not to use your primary light while dressing and preparing equipment, especially if your light is a rechargeable. You will need the full charge for the dive. This is why arriving at dusk, or bringing suitable surface lights, is so important. If you must use a dive light, use the secondary or chemical light.

Figure 4-1   *When night diving, the first step is to set up the surface lights.*

If you are using a flashing light, be aware that in most navigable waters a flashing light at the surface is considered a distress signal. Therefore, check the regulations in your area carefully before using this type of light.

There are two basic types of dive sites, shore and boat, and each requires slightly different surface light preparation.

■ **Shore:** When setting up entry/exit surface lights on shore there are two goals. One goal is to provide adequate lighting for dressing, entering the water, and exiting the water. When carrying equipment from the vehicle, you need enough light to find your way to the dive site. Make several trips rather than trying to carry too much at once, because it is easier to slip and fall in the dark. The other goal is to provide a useful landmark, easily seen from the water, that indicates the way back to shore. There should be two lights, one set up higher than the other in a vertical line. Separating the lights makes them easier to see from a distance, should you need to surface and find the direction back. This will lead the diver right to the exit point by following the vertical line. You can either set up two lights or use a street light combined with your own gas lantern or flashing light. As mentioned earlier, it is a good idea to have someone on shore to watch the lights. That way they will not extinguish during your dive, or be stolen by beach thieves.

Position one light higher than the other ...

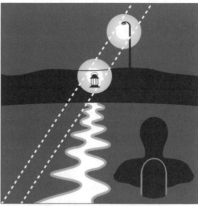

... so they can be lined up as a directional guide.

■ **Boat:** Without lights, you could get disoriented when trying to find the boat, and actually swim away from the boat by mistake (Figure 4-2). Therefore, put up two lights, one higher than the other, just as you would from shore. Of course, boats come equipped with lights, but you run the risk of draining the batteries if you use them as surface lights. It is also a good idea to put a strobe or chemical light on the descent/ascent line and ladder. On a boat, as on the shore, you should have someone on the boat watching the lights.

Figure 4-2 *Surface light on boat.*

ENTERING THE WATER

Entering limited visibility water is not much different than on any other dive. Always use the safest, easiest, least disorienting method. During the day, beaches usually represent a moderate transition. At night, the process can be little trickier. In either case, if the surf is not heavy, walk with your buddy about knee-deep into the water carrying your fins. Stop there and, one buddy at a time, put on your fins. Now walk backwards carefully until you begin to float, turn around, and swim out. When walking in the dark, watch out for things you cannot see in the water.

Entries from rocky shores are more difficult and should not be attempted without first inquiring about the best method from local divers or the local dive store. Do not attempt to enter the water without putting your fins on first. Since moving with fins is very awkward, use caution. Edging toward the water on your bottom, with mask on and regulator in your mouth, is one way. When you reach the water, slip in as gracefully as possible and swim away from the shore. Steep, rocky shores are not good entry points at night because they are too hazardous to negotiate safely in the dark.

When entering the water from a boat, use either the step-in or seated entry. These entries give you the most control and leave you the least disoriented. Do not enter the water carrying lights or cameras. If you are on a chartered boat, the crew should hand you these items. If you are on a private boat, have your buddy pass all accessories to you after you are in the water, then your buddy should enter.

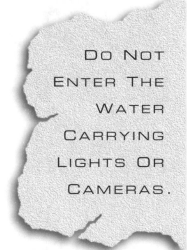

DO NOT ENTER THE WATER CARRYING LIGHTS OR CAMERAS.

After entering the water, you may need to swim to the dive area before descending. This is usually done in favor of swimming along the bottom when a long underwater swim is required. In that case, you would use most of your air simply getting there, so the better alternative is to conserve your air by swimming on the surface. Of course, before making a long surface swim, you need to evaluate possible boat traffic, currents, and your chances of navigating accurately to the dive site (Figure 4-3). Shorter swims are best done underwater, by following the contour of the bottom and using a compass. Obviously, the best time to decide about the swim is during the site selection and dive planning stage.

Figure 4-3 *Evaluate the safety of long surface swims at night.*

DESCENDING

The descent procedures for night and limited visibility diving are very similar to any other dive. Use the procedures taught in your Open Water Diver course. Make sure you and your buddy are both ready before descending, stay close together and proceed at the same pace. Descend slowly and adjust your buoyancy as necessary.

The best way to descend in limited visibility or at night is by using a line. Although not always available, lines work well because you have something stable to hang onto. This helps you judge your speed and can help you slow your descent, if you or your buddy have trouble with ear clearing. It also helps control any disorientation (Figure 4-4). A condition called vertigo or spatial disorientation can occur on descent, and the causes and preventions of these conditions are discussed thoroughly in the next section.

When using a line, do not descend until both you and your buddy are ready, then descend feet-first and facing your buddy. Use your left hand to control the automatic inflator, and your right hand to hang onto the line or to check your instruments.

If no line is available, the key is to stay close to your buddy. To do so, do not start until both you and your buddy are ready, then descend slowly and at the same pace. Use your left hand to control the automatic inflator. Use your right hand to monitor your instruments and, if one of you has trouble clearing ears or becomes disoriented, to grab onto your buddy's BC to maintain contact.

Figure 4-4 *A line will help you control your descent and prevent disorientation.*

When night diving, make sure to double-check your primary and secondary lights before beginning the descent. They should not have leaked, and the beams should be strong. Use your light to "charge" luminescent instruments by holding the light directly on the gauge faces. On the descent, shine your lights downward to avoid "crash landing" on anything, and to prevent shining the light into your buddy's eyes by accident.

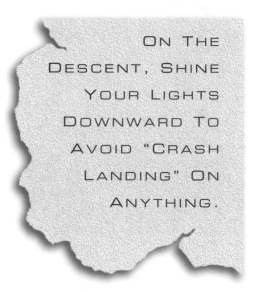

ON THE DESCENT, SHINE YOUR LIGHTS DOWNWARD TO AVOID "CRASH LANDING" ON ANYTHING.

THE DIVE

A variety of night and limited visibility dives were discussed in Chapter 1. Photography, wreck diving and game collecting are just a few. The skills that are particular to night and limited visibility dives are covered in this section. As mentioned earlier, an important factor is spatial disorientation and vertigo, and how they affect your sense of balance under water. The skill of using lights is critical at night, while staying with your buddy is a fundamental skill that is used on every limited visibility dive. More in-depth information on situations that may happen during the dive is available in Chapter 5: Advanced Techniques.

Spatial Disorientation and Vertigo

Spatial disorientation and vertigo can occur on descent, during the dive, or on ascent. They are a large part of the psychological aspect of night and limited visibility diving. Spatial disorientation is a discrepancy between movement the eyes perceive and what is actually occurring. Vertigo is an unnerving phenomenon of feeling movement, but not being able to gauge mentally the speed or direction of the movement. Many divers experiencing vertigo report dizziness, an unpleasant "whirling" sensation, a lightheadedness, even a nauseating motion sickness. In either case, the inability to gauge movement correctly is responsible for divers descending when they thought they were ascending, and for descending and ascending too fast. It is also an unwanted source of stress.

There are a variety of causes for spatial disorientation and vertigo. The main reason is your ear. In common terms, the ear is divided into three parts: the outer ear, the middle ear, and the inner ear. Cold water entering your outer ear can cause disorientation until the water is warmed. If an

Common Causes of Disorientation & Vertigo

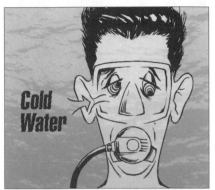

Cold water can cause disorientation.

Unequal amounts of water enter
left and right outer ears.

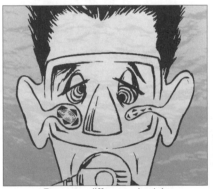

Pressure difference in right
and left Middle ears.

When upside-down, the inner ear is at an
angle that can cause vertigo.

unequal amount of water enters the left and right outer ears it can lead to vertigo, because it disrupts the balance in the outer ear. This can stem from anything that restricts water from entering the ears. Examples are a hood not allowing proper water flow, and a buildup of ear wax.

Another common cause of vertigo is pressure difference in the right and left middle ears. This can happen on descent or ascent. On descent, it is due to unequal or inadequate equalization. If this happens, you should ascend until the condition subsides, then try again slowly. On ascent, it occurs because the air releasing from the automatic opening of your Eustachian tubes is unequal or inadequate. Something, such as mucous, may have blocked the tube's opening. This is also called a "reverse block." If this happens, you should descend until you feel better, then try ascending slowly.

Descending head-first can also cause vertigo. In this position, the inner ear is at an angle which tends to produce vertigo. It can also occur during the dive if you are hanging upside down, looking underneath a rock. Anytime you are inverted and feel disoriented, simply assume an upright position, control your breathing, and the feeling should pass quickly.

Descending too quickly at night or in limited visibility without a line can cause spatial disorientation. It is similar to being on a very fast carnival ride; your senses have difficulty discerning the speed without references. To avoid descending too fast, which is easy to do as the air compresses in your BC and wet suit, add small amounts of air to your BC as needed for neutral buoyancy. The recommended rate of descent is the rate you feel comfortable with, not to exceed 75 feet (23 metres) per minute.

In general, the best methods for controlling spatial disorientation and vertigo are to use a line when descending and ascending, and to descend feet-first. If you are not using a line and you become disoriented, one good method to combat it is to study your depth gauge (Figure 4-5). It gives you something to focus on, and allows you to judge your speed. Staying close to your buddy also helps avoid vertigo, because he or she provides a reference point. If you get confused as to which way is up, watch your bubbles or put your hand into the bubble exhaust stream from your regulator. Bubbles always go towards the surface.

Figure 4-5   *Should you become disoriented, one good method to combat it is to study your depth gauge.*

Using Lights

Lights can be used either at night or during the day, however, the techniques differ slightly. This section discusses both situations, plus a lighting problem called "scatter."

■ **Scatter:** If the water is clear, you can point the light directly at any object, except your buddy's face. In limited visibility, hold the light above or to the side of the object you are illuminating so the beam points at an angle. This will provide better results because the water contains suspended particles, which reduces your range of vision by "blocking your view." Your light illuminates the suspended particles and creates "scatter." Scatter interferes with visibility because light reflects off the suspended particles back to the source (Figure 4-6). Near the bulb a "hot spot" is created because that is where light is the brightest. This hot spot is the source of the most distracting scatter. By holding the light at arms length and at an angle, the hot spot and the majority of the illuminated suspended particles are out of your line of vision. This maximizes the light cast onto the object and minimizes the effect of scatter.

Figure 4-6

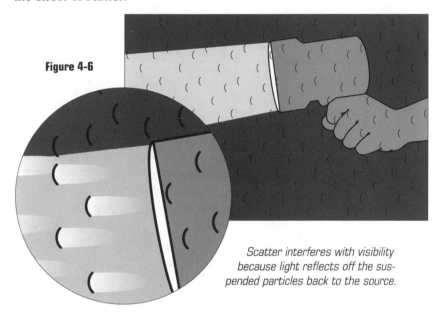

Scatter interferes with visibility because light reflects off the suspended particles back to the source.

This is similar to how car headlight beams work in rain or snow storms at night. Often the low beams provide better visibility than the high beams, because they reflect less light off the rain or snow particles (scatter) near the headlight, and more off objects from a distance, such as oncoming cars. This has to do with the angle and intensity of the beam.

■ **Night Diving:** The most important rule of using lights is, *never shine your light in your buddy's eyes!* If you have ever had your picture taken and looked at the flash as it went off, you have some idea about the implications. Remember, dive lights are extremely bright,

NEVER SHINE YOUR LIGHT IN YOUR BUDDY'S EYES!

far brighter than almost any household light. One direct glance into a dive light could blind your buddy for several minutes. Not being able to see under water is scary at best, and dangerous at worst.

If you want to get your buddy's attention, the proper way is to shine the light at his or her body. You and your buddy may even devise a set of communication signals. Examples are switching the light on and off, or flashing it quickly back and forth in an up and down or circular motion.

On descent, point your light downward so you can see below you. On ascent, point your light upward so you can see above you. This will let you see if you are going to bump into anything. If the visibility is limited, correct for scatter as described above.

You can use your light to communicate with your buddy at night.

■ **Limited Visibility:** Using lights in limited visibility does not improve visibility. They are used either to return light at depth, or to revive color. The suspended particles that cause the turbid water are still present and highlighted scatter is the result. The narrower the beam of the light, the greater distance it will penetrate, while minimizing scatter.

Staying With Your Buddy

Another important part of diving at night or in limited visibility is to stay with your buddy. Under these conditions, buddies are more difficult to keep track of, and losing a buddy usually means surfacing to find him or her. This is not a big problem if the dive is shallow. However, on deep or repetitive dives, going up and down can be dangerous.

How closely you keep track of your buddy is largely a function of the visibility (Figure 4-7). The lower the visibility, the closer you need to stay together, and the more frequently you need to check for his or her presence. Another factor is how well you know your buddy. You will probably check more often the first time you dive with a buddy. However, the more you dive together, the more you should watch for complacency. That is, don't assume your buddy is keeping track of you, or that your buddy is ok because she normally is.

Figure 4-7 *How closely you keep track of your buddy is largely a function of the visibility.*

There are several ways of staying in contact besides swimming elbow to elbow. At night, you can watch your buddy's primary or chemical light. In limited visibility, an effective tether is for each buddy to hold onto a short rope, or buddy line. It allows mobility and still maintains contact. Another method is to hold your buddy's hand, or hang onto his console. Staying in the same position relative to your buddy throughout the dive will also work to keep the team together. This also reduces the constant buddy checks to see if they are still next to you.

One method of maintaining contact is holding hands.

ASCENDING

On ascent, you have most of the same considerations as on descent, however, there are other factors such as rate of ascent and safety stops. Disorientation and vertigo can occur during ascent, affecting your ability to judge direction, and possibly making you miscalculate your rate of ascent. The main concern is that you might ascend faster than the recommended rate of 30 feet (9 metres) per minute.

As on descent, lines are valuable tools for ascending. They make it easier for buddies to stay together, help prevent control disorientation and vertigo, control the rate of ascent, and are useful for safety stops. When using a line in limited visibility, either during the day or at night, use standard ascent procedures. Do not begin the ascent until both you and your buddy are ready. Face your buddy, and use your left hand to vent air from your BC to maintain the proper rate of ascent. Use your right hand to hang onto the line, or to monitor the ascent rate by watching your depth gauge or computer.

Without a line the ascent is trickier, but the technique is similar. Again, do not start until you and your buddy are ready. You should establish slight positive buoyancy to make sure you head towards the surface. With your left hand, vent air from your BC to maintain the proper ascent rate. With your right hand, watch your depth gauge or computer to monitor the ascent rate. Stay together in the event that one of you has a problem, and if you need to establish contact, grab your buddy's BC with your right hand. This means you will be switching the right hand from your instruments to his BC, as needed.

Rate of Ascent

In limited visibility, during the day and at night, it is very difficult to judge how fast you are ascending without using a depth gauge and timing device or a computer (Figure 4-8). At the recommended rate of 30 feet or 9 metres per minute, you need to ascend one-half foot or .15 metres per second.

Figure 4-8   *It is very difficult to judge how fast you're ascending without using a depth gauge or computer.*

Safety Stops

It is well documented that a safety stop for 3 minutes at 15 feet (5 minutes at 5 metres) greatly decreases nitrogen absorbed during the dive. Therefore, a safety stop is recommended on any dive deeper than 30 feet (9 metres).

If you are diving from a boat, there are usually one or more lines available for a safety stop. Drop bars work particularly well (Figure 4-9). Any line makes it easier to maintain a constant depth, especially if the water is rough or a current is present.

If you are making a safety stop without the aid of a line, be aware of currents. During a safety stop, a current can push you quite a distance.

Figure 4-9   *Drop bars work well when making safety stops on boats.*

One way to make a safety stop in a current without a line is to swim towards the exit point while maintaining a 15 feet (4.5 metres) depth. This is difficult without a compass, and surfacing to check direction negates the benefit derived from a safety stop.

EXITING THE WATER

The final part of any night dive is getting out of the water safely. Re-entering boats and exiting from shore each have their own unique problems, and require different techniques.

Boats

With boats, your main safety consideration is the movement of the boat due to wave action. Be aware of ladders and platforms as they can bump your head on the downside of a wave. Time your entry to coincide with the lowest point of the wave; it is better to be pulled up by a wave, rather than suddenly dropped by one. Have your buddy hold your light and other accessories, or hand them to a crew member; you will need both hands free to re-enter the boat so you can see the ladder or platform. Someone will need to shine their light for you. Follow the captain's procedure for removing weight belts and fins, but leave your mask on your face and regulator in your mouth until you are safely aboard. If you plan on diving frequently from boats, the SSI Boat Diving specialty course is an excellent way to learn the fundamentals quickly.

Shore

When exiting from the shore, your main considerations are surf and rocky shores. Surf on a beach can be tricky at night. Swim until the water no longer supports your body's weight and, if necessary, crawl on your hands and knees until you are out of the surf. Otherwise, you might be able to stand up. If you choose to stand, be ready to support yourself as the next wave comes; it may send you crashing back into the water. Because of this, you and your buddy should help each other get stable, remove fins and walk to shore. As a rule, you should avoid rocky shores for night diving unless you know the area well, or you scouted a safe exit point. Still, be very cautious. Consider having a friend on shore to help with the exit. They can provide lighting so you can see, plus hold your light and other accessories for you. When exiting in surf or onto a rocky shore, do not remove your mask or regulator until you are out of the water.

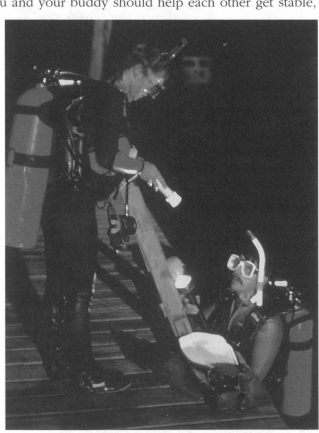

When climbing ladders at night, your buddy can provide light and help with your equipment.

FINISHING THE DIVE

After you are out of the water, get dry and warm as soon as possible (Figure 4-10). It is a good idea to have street clothes and towels handy so you can change right away. At night, hypothermia is a concern because it can be considerably colder than during the day. Of course, it does not occur immediately. The point is, do not take chances by getting chilled.

Figure 4-10   *After you are out of the water, get dry and warm as soon as possible.*

Take Care of Equipment

Taking care of your equipment is the next priority so nothing will be lost or left behind. Pick up all equipment from the dive site and pack it away. Put your equipment into your bag or storage location as soon as possible, to avoid mix-ups with other divers. As soon as you can, wash your equipment with fresh water, and hang it to dry.

Log the Dive

After taking care of your equipment, you should log the dive. As a rule, the sooner you do it the better, and it is best if you do it before leaving the dive site. At the dive site, your buddy is there, and the exciting events and important data are still fresh in your mind. If conditions dictate that you leave the site as soon as possible, try at least to log

Logged dives are an integral part of your Specialty and Advanced Diver certifications.

the dive that evening. The important thing is to do it. Logged dives indicate your Level of Experience (1-10) and recent diving activity. High Levels of Experience qualify you for *Century Diver* (Level 5, 100 dives), *Gold⁵⁰⁰ Diver* (Level 9, 500 dives) and *Platinum¹⁰⁰⁰ Diver* (Level 10, 1000 dives). The highest level is *Platinum Pro⁵⁰⁰⁰ Diver*, which requires 5000 dives.

Logged dives are also an integral part of earning SSI's *Specialty Diver*, *Advanced Open Water Diver* and *Master Diver* ratings. These ratings have the industry's highest requirements, because you must log a certain number of dives before you can qualify. Additional diving, we have found, is the secret to making you a truly advanced diver.

Clean Up

Before leaving, clean up the dive site. If you are on shore, pick up all your trash, beverage cans and food wrappers. Put out bonfires completely, if you started one. Leave the dive site looking as good or better than you found it.

The techniques for diving at night or during the day in limited visibility are similar. The techniques for descending, ascending and navigation are the same. It is largely the addition of lights, and the vastly different diving atmosphere that makes each experience unique. Using lines for control is an excellent safety consideration to either situation. Once you learn to dive in limited visibility, you can concentrate on having fun.

CHAPTER 4
REVIEW

1. The best way to _____ in limited visibility or at night is by using a line.

2. If no line is available, the key is to stay close to your _____ .

3. _____ _____ is a discrepancy between movement the eyes perceive and what is actually occurring.

4. The most important rule of using lights is *never shine your light in your* _____ _____ *!*

5. On descent, point your light _____ so you can see below you. On ascent, point your light _____ so you can see above you.

ADVANCED TECHNIQUES

5

CHAPTER 5:
ADVANCED TECHNIQUES

To become a complete night and limited visibility diver, there are a few additional considerations you should know about. Some are special situations such as lost buddy, light failure, and relocating the boat or shore. The rest are advanced skills such as buoyancy control and navigation. Knowing how to handle the special situations, along with practicing the advanced skills, will make you a more confident and comfortable diver.

This chapter discusses these additional considerations for night and limited visibility diving, which should round out your training and give you the fundamentals to dive in almost any kind of limited visibility condition.

BUOYANCY CONTROL

For several reasons, it is important that you maintain neutral buoyancy during your dive. By staying off the bottom, you avoid kicking up sand and silt (Figure 5-1). This maintains the visibility, which is important on night and limited visibility dives. And, with more and more divers enjoying the underwater world, the challenge of all divers is to impact the

environment as little as possible. By mastering the third dimension, you gain extra control, allowing you to avoid touching, grabbing, and pulling on delicate marine life. Other advantages are slower air consumption and energy conservation.

Diving neutral is one of the most subtle of all skills to master, and it is one indication of an advanced, comfortable diver. Some keys to good buoyancy control are relaxing while under water, proper weighting, and breath control (not breath holding!). It is recommended to seek additional training in buoyancy control, and to practice in a pool whenever possible. Eventually, you will gain the graceful sense of balance and equilibrium that is one of diving's real pleasures.

Figure 5-1 *By staying off the bottom, you avoid kicking up sand and silt.*

NAVIGATION

Another extremely useful skill in night and limited visibility diving is navigating. Navigation saves time, air, and the need to surface for finding direction. With a compass, you can find your way back to the entry point even in very limited visibility or when there are no distinct underwater features (Figure 5-2). During deep or repetitive no-decompression

Figure 5-2 *With a compass, you can find your way back to the entry point even in very limited visibility.*

dives, going up and down to check your location jeopardizes the dive plan calculations.

To find your way, you can use natural navigation, a compass, or a combination of both. Natural navigation uses underwater landmarks as guideposts. Reef formations, unusual rocks and bottom contours all serve as distinguishing landmarks. The floating needle in compasses points north, giving south, east and west directions from this reference point. Divers can either follow a compass course, or swim out in one direction and back in the opposite. Many divers rely on both natural navigation and compasses. While using the compass for direction, they also observe the topography, noting helpful landmarks to guide them as well.

It is useful to judge distance as well as direction. Many divers use a timing device, swimming out for so many minutes in a certain direction, then back for the same time in the opposite direction. Others count the number of fin kicks instead of minutes.

There are other simple tricks of navigation. In general, when the water gets colder, you are going deeper. Another method of determining depth is light. Usually, light fades as depth increases. This is important because depth is often an indication of direction. If you are trying to reach shore, for instance, colder water with less light means you may be headed the wrong way.

There are several procedures for proper navigation. You should orient yourself to the dive site while you are still on the surface. Note the general direction of reefs, kelp, and rock formations. By taking a compass heading, you will know the direction to your destination, and the direction back (Figure 5-3). After your descent, take a moment to re-orient yourself before starting the swim. Then, during the dive, check your direction as frequently as needed to maintain orientation.

This short description was meant to be a general overview. If you have interest in accurate underwater navigation, check into an SSI Navigation specialty course. It will teach you the fundamentals of compasses and using them, as well as natural navigation.

Figure 5-3 *Take a compass heading while still on the surface.*

WHAT TO DO IF YOU LOSE YOUR BUDDY

As with all other unfavorable diving situations, a lost buddy procedure should be discussed during the dive planning stage, as mentioned in Chapter 3. The best approach is a series of logical, predictable actions, each done for a reasonable length of time. The advantage is that you maximize your chances of finding your buddy, without wasting time and energy. The procedures for night and limited visibility diving are very similar.

When you realize your buddy is missing, swim up a few feet. Hold your light straight out and make two 360° turns (Figure 5-4). This will allow you to see your buddy, or your buddy to see you. If you have not located your buddy after 30 seconds, ascend to the surface, your buddy may be waiting for you. Wait for one minute, looking for a light or bubbles that you can follow back down, or for your buddy to surface. If you have not relocated your buddy, there may be trouble. Go back to shore or the boat immediately for help. Make sure you remember where you last saw your buddy, because a search might be necessary. This is not easy to do, but it will greatly aid the search effort.

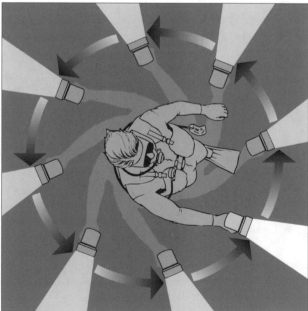

Figure 5-4   *To locate a missing buddy, hold your light straight out and make two 360° turns.*

WHAT TO DO IF YOUR LIGHT GOES OUT (NIGHT DIVING)

Occasionally, a light will flood, or the battery or bulb will fail. This is the reason for recommending a secondary light, staying shallow, and staying close to your buddy.

There are three light failure situations described: 1) when you have a secondary light; 2) when you have no secondary light, but your buddy is nearby; and 3) when you have no secondary light and your buddy is not nearby. You will see that having a secondary light is the easier, safer situation.

With a Secondary Light

The best way to handle the situation is to have a secondary light. At the time of light failure, you simply switch to the back-up. After that, you and your buddy need to decide whether or not to cancel the dive. The decision should hinge on the size and quality of your secondary light, the size and quality of your buddy's secondary, as well as the water conditions, your comfort level, and your confidence in your buddy. Generally, three lights for two divers is fine, two lights for two divers is marginal, but one light for two divers is unsafe. To make the decision, weigh the factors using common sense and do not hesitate to cancel the dive if either you or your buddy are not comfortable continuing. If you do terminate the dive, end it as normally as possible using all standard ascent procedures, including a safety stop.

A secondary light should be accessible in case of light failure.

No Secondary Light, Buddy Nearby

If you do not have a secondary light, but your buddy is nearby, the situation is more difficult, but in no way an emergency. Your course of action is to inform your buddy, terminate the dive and ascend safely. Do not take the situation lightly, but do not overreact.

When you realize your light is out, inform your buddy. Primarily because of situations like this, you should stay close to your buddy throughout the dive. You can also alert your buddy by banging on your tank with your knife. The next step is to terminate the dive. Without a light, it is completely unwise to continue the dive. The diver with the light is in control, but only proceed when both of you are ready. A slow, controlled ascent is vital, and there is no reason for anything else. After all, the only problem is a failed light. If a line is available, use it. If no line is available, hold onto each other's BC for more control. If possible or if necessary, make a safety stop, but only if it can be done without jeopardizing the ascent. Your main consideration is to reach the surface safely.

No Secondary Light, Buddy Not Nearby

The least desirable situation is when your primary light fails, you have no secondary, and your buddy is not nearby. Searching for your buddy is neither practical nor wise. Basically, you have little choice but to ascend alone. Your challenge will be to ascend as normally and safely as possible. As stated earlier, there is no need to overreact. Remember, the only equipment problem is the light. There are, however, several things that could complicate the situation. Maintaining a clear head is the key to keeping things under control. The first problem is, obviously, the lack of light. It will hinder reading gauges, finding lines, and seeing what is above on ascent. If you cannot read your gauge, it will be difficult to judge the proper ascent rate. Look up at your bubbles to help judge your ascent rate. Try not to ascend faster than your smallest bubbles. To check for obstructions, look up and hold your hand above you. There may be

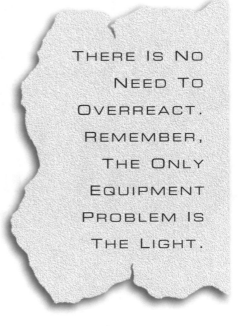

THERE IS NO NEED TO OVERREACT. REMEMBER, THE ONLY EQUIPMENT PROBLEM IS THE LIGHT.

moonlight to help you judge direction and rate of ascent. The second and third problems are vertigo and disorientation. Looking up at your bubbles may help or, if you can, stop and breathe deeply before ascending again. A fourth problem is that, because of the buddy system breakdown, your buddy will be diving alone after your ascent. Hopefully, he or she will initiate lost buddy procedures soon after your ascent, and will arrive on the surface shortly after you do. If not, swim back to the exit point and wait for him or her. Finally, ending the dive normally, including a safety stop, may not be possible if you do not have a line. As stated earlier, your main consideration is to reach the surface safely.

RELOCATING THE BOAT OR SHORE (NIGHT DIVING)

If you are a proficient underwater navigator, it is possible to conduct the entire dive under water, entering and exiting at the same place without surfacing to determine direction. However, many divers are not experienced or confident with a compass, and must surface at least once to determine direction. For those divers, bright surface lights at the exit point are invaluable. They provide a reliable beacon to follow back to the boat or shore.

The value of having two surface lights, one higher than the other, becomes apparent to divers following them back. The higher light over the lower one creates a "pointer" effect. When situated that way, the lights are more visible, can be seen from a greater distance, and are easier to follow.

When using surface lights to relocate the exit point, some divers take a compass heading a few feet (metres) below the surface. Others swim

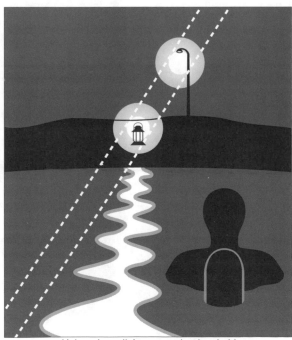

Using shore lights as navigational aid.

on the surface, glancing occasionally at the lights to make sure they are headed in the right direction. The method you use depends largely on your compass skills, the water conditions, the distance back, your air supply and the boat traffic. If there are large, rolling waves, swimming under the water might be calmer. On calm nights where boats are prohibited, swimming on the surface might be more comfortable. If you cannot use a compass, staying close to the shore or boat helps avoid long swims back to the exit point. Mainly, judge the conditions with common sense and use the best method for relocating the boat or shore.

SUMMARY

Limited visibility diving, either during the day or at night, is a natural extension of your diving horizons. Daytime limited visibility offers an abundance of pleasurable, accessible diving locations. It is fun, can be enjoyed frequently and inexpensively, and the variety of activities is unsurpassed. With a light in the nighttime water, you can visit a completely different world. Not only that, the already enjoyable weightless

sensation is enhanced indescribably by the added dimension of darkness. All limited visibility diving presents new challenges, such as vertigo and spatial disorientation. To overcome these new challenges, new techniques are taught in this course. After completing this course, you will understand the fundamentals needed to begin exploring the underwater world in almost any kind of limited visibility condition. After that, it is up to you to dive smart, be safety conscious, plan well, know your limits, and dive within them.

Diving at night opens up a whole new world!

CHAPTER 5
REVIEW

1. With a _____, you can find your way back to the entry point even in very limited visibility or when there are no distinct underwater features.

2. In general, when the water gets colder, you are going _____.

3. At the time of _____ failure, you simply switch to the backup.

4. The value of having two surface lights, one higher than the other, becomes apparent to divers following them back. The higher light over the lower one creates a "_____" effect.

5. After completing this course, you will understand the fundamentals needed to begin exploring the underwater world in almost any kind of _____ _____ condition.

APPENDIX

1
Equipment Checklist

2
Spare Parts/Repair Kit Checklist

APPENDIX 1

Night/Limited Visibility Diving
Equipment Checklist

- ☐ Mask
- ☐ Snorkel & Keeper
- ☐ Fins
- ☐ Diving Suit
- ☐ Boots
- ☐ Gloves
- ☐ Hood
- ☐ Weight System
- ☐ Weights
- ☐ Buoyancy Compensator
- ☐ Tank(s) Full
- ☐ Regulator
- ☐ Alternate Air Source
- ☐ Pressure Gauge
- ☐ Timing Device
- ☐ Depth Gauge
- ☐ Compass
- ☐ Knife
- ☐ Whistle
- ☐ Dive Computer
- ☐ Thermometer
- ☐ Defogging Solution
- ☐ Dive Light/Batteries
- ☐ Chemical Light
- ☐ Dive Flag

- ☐ Dive Tables
- ☐ Log Book
- ☐ Certification Card
- ☐ Speargun
- ☐ Extra Points
- ☐ Goody Bag
- ☐ Fishing License
- ☐ U/W Camera
- ☐ Flash or Strobe
- ☐ Batteries
- ☐ Film
- ☐ Slate
- ☐ Spare Parts Kit
- ☐ Swim Suit
- ☐ Towels
- ☐ Suntan Lotion/Sunscreen
- ☐ First Aid Kit
- ☐ Money for Emergency Calls
- ☐ Money for Air Fills
- ☐ Money for Galley & Tips
- ☐ Passport
- ☐ _____
- ☐ _____
- ☐ _____

APPENDIX 2

Night/Limited Visibility Diving
Spare Parts/Repair Kit

☐ Fin Straps & Buckles

☐ Mask Straps & Buckles

☐ Snorkel Keeper

☐ Knife Retaining Kit

☐ Knife Leg Strap

☐ Needle and Thread

☐ CO_2 Cartridges

☐ O-rings, Bulb for Light

☐ Batteries

☐ Dust Cap

☐ Regulator Port Plug

☐ Regulator Mouthpiece and Cable Ties

☐ O-rings

☐ Silicone Spray

☐ Silicone Grease

☐ Wetsuit Cement

☐ BC Patch Kit

☐ Buckles for BC

☐ Buckle for Weight Belt

☐ Screwdriver (Straight & Phillips)

☐ Pliers

☐ Crescent Wrench

☐ 5/32-Inch Allen Wrench

☐ WD-40®

☐ _____

☐ _____

☐ _____

☐ _____

☐ _____

☐ _____